D0524303

-8

ι 8

2

25 ι

Sch

First published in 2008
by Franklin Watts

Text © Shaun Hutson and Deborah Smith 2008
Illustrations © John Charlesworth 2008
Cover design by Peter Scoulding

Franklin Watts
338 Euston Road
London NW1 3BH

Franklin Watts Australia
Level 17/207 Kent Street
Sydney, NSW 2000

A CIP catalogue record for this book
is available from the British Library.

ISBN: 978 0 7496 7716 9

Printed in Great Britain

Franklin Watts is a division of Hachette Children's Books,
an Hachette Livre UK company.

Evil Ink

Spike T. Adams

Illustrated by John Charlesworth

W
FRANKLIN WATTS
LONDON•SYDNEY

Chapter 1

Easy.

Piece of piss.

None of them see me take the console.

Only that fat guard.

And he has no chance of catching me.

"STOP!" he shouts.

Like I'm going to.

I look back to see the fat guard is losing ground.

"Stop you little bastard!" he shouts.

Eat shit, fat boy.

I get to Jordan's place.

"Yo, Craig," I say. "Is Jordan in?"

"Yeah, with the others," he tells me. "What ya got?"

I show him the box.

"Jordan will be well pleased when he sees this," I say.

Craig shrugs. "Maybe," he says. "Go in and find out."

So I do.

I hold out the box to Jordan.

"Look what I got," I say to him.

"I had one of them for months, man," Raymond says. "They is weak."

"Weak," says Conor. Like he's a parrot.

He punches my arm.

"Leave him alone, Conor," Jordan says.

But he still gives me back the box.

I'm gutted.

"Youz two gonna help me and my old man tonight?" he asks the others.

"All that skunk and blow don't shift itself."

"Sure, man," Raymond says.

"What about it, Tommy-boy?" Conor asks me.

My face burns.

"My mum's on night shift," I say. "Gotta look after my little sister."

When they laugh at me, it hurts real bad.

"Ya pussy," says Raymond.

"Pussy," Conor agrees.

They're always getting at me.

Anyway, I don't wanna help shift gear.

My dad died on smack.

Jordan stands up and stretches.

We all look at the new tattoo on his back.

"Bwoy, that new tattoo is a killer, bro!"
Raymond says.

Jordan grins. "Yeah. Hurt like a bitch."

"How long it take?" Conor asks.

"About six hours," Jordan tells him.

"Shit! That prove ya ain't no pussy!" Raymond says.

"Maybe ya should get one, Tommy-boy," Conor tells me, with a laugh.

The others laugh too.

"Yeah," I say.

And I mean it.

Coz nobody is gonna call me pussy again.

Chapter 2

Next Saturday morning, I'm standing in *Dream Tattoo*.

Hidden away in a back street.

The other tattoo places turned me away.

They said I was too young.

But Eve just smiles.

"What's your name?" she asks.

"Tom," I say. My face feels hot.

I feel a bit shy. Coz she's well fit.

"What kinda tattoo do you want, Tom?" she asks.

"I want…" I can't say it.

But Eve seems to know.

She says it for me. "You want a tattoo that will bring you respect, don't you Tom?"

"Yeah," I say, amazed.

Eve smiles. "Trust me," she says. "I'll give you what you want."

So I do.

Bwoy! It kills, getting a tattoo.

I have it on my back, like Jordan.

His looks well cool.

Plus, I figure Mum won't see it there.

She won't like me getting a tattoo.

But Jordan and the others will be well impressed.

"It's done," Eve tells me.

I see it in the mirror.

It's a work of art. A demon. Even better than Jordan's.

I'm speechless.

"Nobody will mess with you now," she says.

"Have ya done one like this before?" I ask her.

Eve smiles. "This is a one-off.

I only do custom jobs," she tells me.

I hand over the money.

Can't wait to show Jordan and the others.

See what they got to say.

Chapter 3

I find Jordan and the rest of the crew at
the park.

I pull off my shirt and jog over to join in the game.

Jordan spots it first. He comes over for a
closer look.

"Shit, man, that's a wicked tattoo," he says.

"Yeah – respect, man," says Craig. "Must have
taken hours."

"Guess Tommy-boy ain't no pussy," Raymond
admits.

Conor nods.

Respect. It feels so great.

I feel bigger. Stronger.

I'm gonna get that ball and nobody is gonna
stop me.

I take the ball from Conor.

First time ever.

I feel strong enough to kick a hole in a wall.

"Take it easy, man!" Jordan calls.

"Ya could have hurt him bad, man!" shouts Raymond.

Conor says nothing. Just limps off to the bench.

Who's the pussy now?

I score.

Then I score some more.

Chapter 4

That night, I smile as I look at my tattoo.

I wash it — then put on the cream that Eve gave me to help it heal.

I'm still buzzing.

I got respect. About time.

But man, my skin itches.

Feels like something's crawling under it.

Under the tattoo.

Like ants.

No pain.

Just itching...

I get no sleep.

I put on more of Eve's cream.

But nothing kills the itch.

And now I think the skin is infected.

It's all swollen – makes the demon look bigger.

I want to tell Mum – but I can't.

Mum leaves for work.

I have to watch Jamie-Lee.

But the itch is making me mad.

I feel like a caged animal.

I have to get out!

"Stay here. I'll be back soon," I tell Jamie-Lee.

She looks up. "Mum said you have to stay in with me."

I kiss my teeth. "I told ya, I won't be long!" I say.

"And don't be snooping in my room when I'm gone!" I warn her.

"Didn't expect to see you, Tom," Conor says.

I shrug — try not to think about leaving Jamie-Lee on her own.

"And ya didn't expect to get ya arse kicked at football either," I say sharply.

The others laugh.

"So what's going down today?" I ask Jordan.

"Gotta do some collecting for my old man," he tells me.

"Collecting what?" I ask.

"Money — from a customer who ain't too keen on paying," Jordan says.

I scratch my back. "I'm up for that," I say.

The others look at me, surprised.

"Yeah," I say. "Let's go."

Chapter 5

"Hi, Jordan, who's your friend?" asks the guy. "Isn't he a bit small for a bodyguard?"

The guy sounds like a smart-ass to me.

Jordan just smiles. "Ya owe fifty notes, Andy," he says.

"And my dad wants it now."

"Yeah, right..." Andy says with a yawn. "I don't know if I've got it on me."

"Ya'd better look then," Jordan tells him. "We'll help ya."

He pushes Andy inside and we follow.

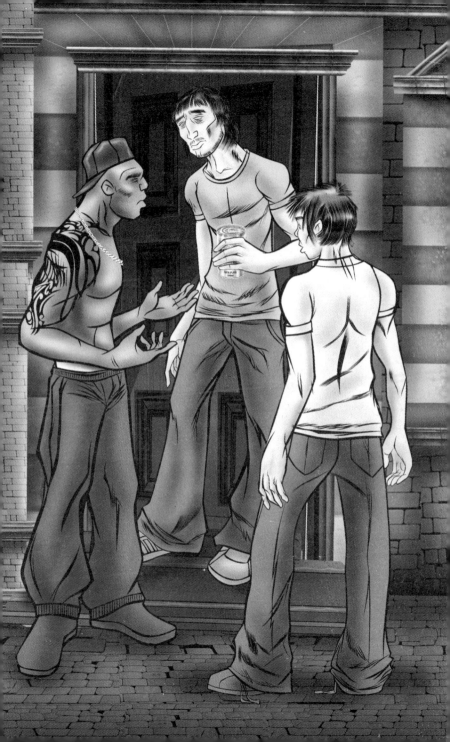

Andy grins. "Sorry, Jordan," he says. "I told you. You'll have to come back some other time."

I look at the guitar in the corner.

"Ya could sell the guitar to get money," I say.

"Yeah, right..." Andy says with a sneer. "That guitar's worth more than you are."

I feel a wave of heat sweep up my back.

No one talks to me like that.

Not any more.

I'm on him. Before he can blink.

Before he knows what's happening.

I only stop when I hear something break.

"Now get the money!" I shout.

"I told you! I haven't got it!" Andy shouts back.

I grab him around the throat.

"Tom, leave him, man," Jordan says. "It's only fifty notes."

"No!" I hiss. "He's gotta pay!"

"Alright, alright!" Andy croaks. "I can find the money. Just get this freak off me!"

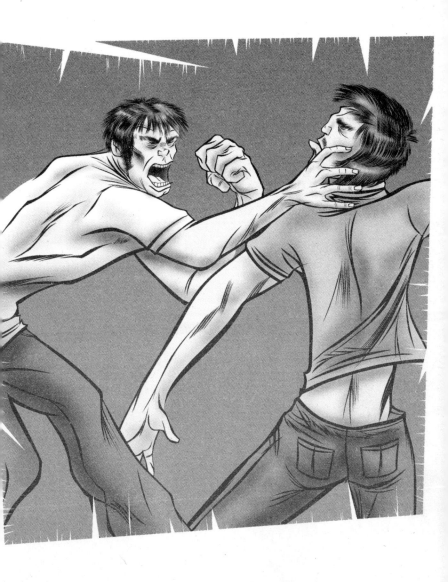

We hook up with the others back at Jordan's.

He tells them what went down at Andy's.

"Ya turning into a real bad ass, Tom," Jordan tells me with a smile.

"Yeah — watch out!" I joke.

I'm laughing with them.

It's great — feeling part of the crew.

But inside, I feel a bit sick.

I don't know what made me hit Andy.

I could have killed him.

It was like I was somebody else for a while.

I think of Jamie-Lee home alone.

Mum will be back from work soon.

"Gotta go, guys," I say.

Don't even finish my can.

Chapter 6

When I get back, Jamie-Lee is upstairs.

In my room.

On my computer.

The hot rage sweeps up my back again.

I see red.

I go over and drag her out.

"Tom! You're hurting me!" she yells.

"What did I tell ya?" I shout at her.

She stumbles to the floor. Curls up into a ball. "Please don't hurt me any more!" she begs, crying.

But I don't care.

"Go in my room again and I'll kill ya!" I roar.

"Tom! What the hell do you think you're doing?"

Mum comes up the stairs.

I didn't hear her come in.

"Don't you dare hurt her!" she yells at me.

"What is WRONG with you?"

She pulls Jamie-Lee to her and pushes me away.

"Your dad was like this — when he was high on smack," she tells me. "Shouting and pushing me about..."

And she starts to cry.

I go into my room and shut the door.

What IS wrong with me?

First that Andy guy — and now my own sister!

It's not like me. Hurting people.

The itching has stopped.

Now the tattoo feels burning hot.

I lie on my bed — and then sit up again.

Something just moved *in* my back.

I stand up and go over to the mirror.

My heart is beating fast.

It happens again.

Something moving, in my back.

This time I can see it, under my shirt.

I tear the shirt off.

As I watch, the demon turns its head.

Looks at me.

I feel like I'm gonna throw up.

Pass out.

The tattoo is alive!

It's taking over.

I feel like I'm gonna go mental.

I know what I have to do.

Get rid of it.

Kill it.

Or I'll end up killing someone.

Maybe my sister.

Or my mum.

Gotta get rid of it now.

Before it's too late.

Chapter 7

Shit! Shit! Shit! It hurts so much.

My back feels on fire.

So much blood.

Can't stop.

Got to cut it away.

But it keeps moving.

Moving away from the knife.

Oh, God. It's screaming.

It knows I'm trying to kill it.

I can't do it.

Eve will have to help me.

No one else can.

I cover myself up.

Wash away the blood.

Hurry down town.

Eve is about to lock up.

I beg her to let me in, so she does.

"Look!" I say. I show her the tattoo.

"Ya got to take it away!"

She smiles. "But it's given you what you wanted, Tom," she says.

She reaches out a hand.

Strokes the demon's head.

It makes a purring noise.

Eve laughs and licks my blood off her fingers.

The tip of her tongue is like the demon's.

She takes off her shades.

Her eyes are like the demon's too.

I don't even think.

Just pick up a knife from the table.

Stab it into her heart.

She staggers back.

Then falls to the floor.

Dead.

The demon screeches.

My back burns.

I feel my skin rip.

The demon claws its way out of me.

And then leaps onto Eve.

It pushes its head into her wound.

Disappears inside her.

Like a rat slipping into a hole.

I pick up my clothes, turn and run.

Chapter 8

I stay in that night.

Watch the news.

Wait for them to talk about the murder.

But no one says anything.

Not one word.

Same the next day.

And the next.

What is happening?

I have to know.

I go back.

Look in the window.

Eve is there. As if nothing has happened.

She sees me.

Smiles.

And then she turns.

I see the tattoo on her back.

My demon.

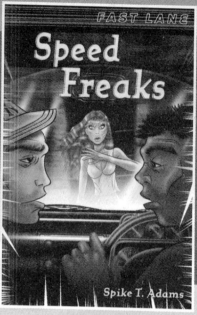